Artificial
LIFE

ZEINAB ARJAH

BALBOA.
PRESS

A DIVISION OF HAY HOUSE

Balboa Press books may be ordered through booksellers or by contacting:

Balboa Press
A Division of Hay House
1663 Liberty Drive
Bloomington, IN 47403
www.balboapress.com.au
1 (877) 407-4847

Because of the dynamic nature of the Internet, any web addresses or
links contained in this book may have changed since publication and
may no longer be valid. The views expressed in this work are solely those
of the author and do not necessarily reflect the views of the publisher,
and the publisher hereby disclaims any responsibility for them.

The author of this book does not dispense medical advice or prescribe the use
of any technique as a form of treatment for physical, emotional, or medical
problems without the advice of a physician, either directly or indirectly. The
intent of the author is only to offer information of a general nature to help you
in your quest for emotional and spiritual well-being. In the event you use any
of the information in this book for yourself, which is your constitutional right,
the author and the publisher assume no responsibility for your actions.

Print information available on the last page.

ISBN: 978-1-4525-3159-5 (sc)
ISBN: 978-1-4525-3160-1 (e)

Balboa Press rev. date: 12/04/2015

Contents

A Glimpse of Horror

14/11/2014

1

I have always wished you were here to keep me company.
I also wished you were here to make me feel less lonely.
Every time you were close by me, I sensed the feeling of being a little more alive.

Then after you left, I felt like an iceberg for a long while.
When you took the first step out of my life,
I couldn't imagine myself without you
Despite all the fighting we endured that night.
If only I could hold onto you so tight
To unveil how much I really love you inside.

It's been a while since I've called you with all my passion
It was ugly to witness that you weren't into my fashion.
My fashion for you was giving love through hidden expressions,
But your idea in fashion was giving love through breaking hearts and ego impressions.

I told you to be patient, and it'll be just fine,
But you left me out of your mind,
Way behind.
How could you even dare
To throw everything I left aside?
How could I be such an idiot to fall back into your eyes?

Baby, I should have learnt the first time I fell outside your mind,
But you just blew me away with words you knew you were able to bribe me with.
And yet I believed every word that came out of your mouth.

And because I'm such a fool,
I can't forget you.
I can't leave you
Or hurt you.
I believed in love at first sight,
But now as we reach the end, I'm starting to feel that nothing is right,
Knowing that love is made to break us
And we are put on earth to fight.

2
There is always a wild side to an innocent face,
But that wasn't really what mattered in this case.
You told me you were going to stand by my side with every strength you had.
Where are you now?
Don't for a second think I'm mad.

If you're going to take this personally,
Well, maybe take a second and look back.
I remember the day you told me not to focus on yesterday because tomorrow might not come.
But hey, I'm here right now, begging for that last day to come.

Really?
You're going to leave for good?
How about the heart you tore apart?
What about all those broken promises you lied about?
How about all my scars you cherished for a while?
I might as well just pull the trigger while you aim the gun at my heart.

You think I wasn't patient enough?
No, listen here.
I prayed for a whole while and asked God to keep you protected from the wild.
I cried myself to sleep most of the time.

After the fights we had late at night,
"I was asleep," you'd always reply.
No, my mama didn't raise me to buy these lies.

I might love shopping, but I will never buy your bullshit.
Without hesitation, you just forget me?
No.
Listen here, mate:
My life began to end the day we became so silent about things
that mattered to us.

You told me this was for the best,
But how could you leave and not take your memories with you?
Remember when your heart betrayed you and you ended up
blaming it on your eyes?
I'll tell you what life taught me?
It's like riding a bicycle:
To keep your balance, you must keep moving.

Now what?
I tell ya—I'm moving on.
Whatcha gonna do?
Oh yeah, that's right—
Blame everything you did on me.
Stop acting like a fool.

I put you too high up in the sky, and I put you there so you
wouldn't be touched by anyone except me.
Not until stones were thrown at you.
I was that shining star; you asked for help afterward.
Well, too bad, moon.
I guess you have to do it on your own from now on.
You always complained about those two stones and what you
did with them.

I advised you to stay away from them.
You agreed for a while,
But I guess you collected that ugly stone with both your hands
and dropped that shining star without taking one last glance.

You claimed you were innocent, and gave bad reputations to those stones.
Wow. That shows how much of a worthy thing you are.
If you could change things, would you?
Oh, that's right:
You're still bragging about how depressed you are for doing stupid things in your life.

Yet I kept telling you the rule for forgetting things was not to look back.
But hell no.
Can somebody tell me which bad boy doesn't like to break the rules?
Yeah, that wasn't him for sure.
Now I can sit here for as long as I want and watch you walk out that door.
I'm going to cry less and be happy more.

Shadow of Haunting

25/01/14

Far away,
I can see your shadow standing right on top of mine.
I hear those nasty voices bringing me down.
You can say all you want; I will remain standing still and try not
to cry,
Emotionally fighting a battle in my heart and haunted mind,
Sacrificing my time for you and your corruptive life.

I am not going to make the most for you anymore, because I
have God right by my side.
You hurting me like that is not what's so called right.
You bring me down with your words and claim it was only a joke.
If I were to joke just like that about you, I wonder how you would
feel?

Take a deep breath and sit yourself down.
I need some time, a little space to figure this out!
My haunting memories keep me up.
I say, "Daddy, please help me. Take me out of this mess. Anyone,
please!"
But Daddy doesn't even know half the things I've been going
through.
He sits aside and says, "This is life, and you will have to learn how
to deal."

I cry, "Daddy, please. I can't do this all alone!
I need you to give me your shoulder, Daddy, I need you to hear
me cry out all that's in my soul!"
Surrounded by many, and yet I'm feeling so alone.
Daddy, I miss Mummy. Please, why won't you help?
Help me out of this trap.
I feel lonely and mad.

I've given up too many times, but I thank Aunty for being there.
She swung her hand in mine as she was falling down her own
traps. But Daddy, I need you because later on I'll either be six feet
down or married to a random man.
I just think it's a little crazy how much I crave your love.
I need your love, Dad. Please show it to me.
It's not easy, Daddy. I barely see my mother anymore.
I feel like you murder me every time you give me that last look.
It's painful, looking at my father's eyes from time to time.
I cried many years, still suffering from one and other.
There are people who don't leave me.
As I cry, they tease me and then claim my tears are all lies.
My own blood hates me, and I don't even understand why.

2
Brother, I'm sorry if I ever made you feel disliked.
I'm here for you. though.
Bear with me if I'm a little mad.
I'm sorry I take it out all on you; it's only so normal, but I'm not glad.
It's just that I've been hurting.
I know that one day we will both get out of this together.
Keep it locked and chained in your heart forever.

I don't want you going through what I've been suffering from for
years.
Keep your trust in us. I love you, and I'll provide you with all your
needs.
If Mum and Dad aren't here, and you feel alone,
I'll be just a heartbeat away.
If you ever need someone who understands you the most,
Just pray.
Raise your hands and ask God to give you another blessing day.

Thank him for giving you the health of what another soul is trying
to fight for.
You may feel a little pressure. I swear I still have your back; that's
for sure.
Remember, our mother and father love us. but it's just hard for
them at times.
Open your hands and speak what's on your mind
God is watching everything you have dug inside.

Unbury the things that keep you far away from who you really are.
If you feel like blood doesn't like you, I feel you because I feel the same way.
I'll be your blood, your bones, and your strength any day.
Float, and believe me, you will not drown.
This is life's concept, constantly bringing us down.

For all the ones I love: I will keep you tied to my heart.
I'm sorry if I ever hurt you in this life.
I never intend on sinning, but it can happen in the blink of an eye.
We go through our ups and downs, but it's only normal for things that are close to one another and beat so fast.
For all the people who believe in me and show support to the very end,
I'd take a bullet for you—not pretend.

At times blood is the reason why I might have to face the trigger.
But one day, I will be in the perfect figure.
Y'all haters hating on what you don't have,
I assure you that y'all don't have mercy in the palm of your hand.
Instead, you wear ugly stains covered with rotten Band-Aids.
Then you ask yourself why it turns out to look that bad,
But you never seem to get it.

You hurt me, but you don't seem to feel it!
Go find something better to do in life.
Set your goals and preach to one another.
Y'all think I'm crazy and weird?
I'll tell you a little something:
I'm limited-edition bitch.

Oh, but please remember to stop copying me.
A wise man once said, "An original is worth more than a copy."
I hear you want to be like me.
Stop right there.
You are nowhere near another me.

The Sin That Got Me Hooked in the Flame That Was Thirsty Again

14/05/14

1
I was on a journey one day.
Out of the blue and into the flame,
As it reached out, it sucked me in.
Knew I got caught from a sin,
And from then nothing was the same.

Just like we put the bird in the cage because its guilt is beauty,
These flames had me in like they were thirsty.
I've been begging them for a while to let me go
I didn't want them to get the best of me, you know.
I can barely breathe in here; it's like there is a knife entering my
soul.
So tired of the blames I've been here for.
My heart is so weak it can barely take such a thing to grow.

It's been through drama, lies, way more than just tears.
And yet cheers to the teenage years.
Do I have to be fierce to the nature of normal I live in?
It's been getting the best of me ever since,
But now it's the flame that burnt another hole in my heart,
And this is just the beginning of a new start.

I grew up playing the role of being rock strong,
Even though I know it's not the end of the battle, because I've
won many times before.
I still feel the struggle though—that's for sure.
And again I repeat a voice in the back of my head.
It was just a broken promise instead.

2
I'm yelling, Free me!
Free me till the day I die.
I've got troubles and many things that I've left behind.
This sin isn't even worth the flame in mind.
I need to breathe, but in this case I'd rather fight.
My back is covered in knives that friends left behind.

When they need me, they treat me like Queen Zee.
And when they're needy,
They praise me and my money tree.
Then after they have their hands on my property,
They call it off like it was a catastrophe.
Nobody dies a virgin, because life stuffs us up,
But it did teach me to be brave and toughen up.

It's deadly when I keep things locked in my heart.
I'd rather draw my feelings and let them dwell apart.
Some people tease me because they just don't get my piece
of art,
But I swear to God it takes a piece of heart and mind
To understand where my scream is booming from.
Daddy, believe me, it was life that brought me up
Into this lady who thought she was always in the wrong.

I'm the Moon's Reflection

12/6/14

1

Groups of people tried to put my life together.
It turns out to be a puzzle with a missing piece;
A mystery had left the puzzle incomplete.

While others made assumptions,
They clearly didn't think this through.
I am a young lady who managed to grow up with a load of talk
from all the haters—and a few loved ones too.

Good people turned into bad because they both had things in
common:
High brands with low education.
So obviously I have had experience with snakes and ladders.

They showed me no love even though I was pleading for some.
I'm a young lady who needed specific attention but clearly didn't
receive it.

Both parents moved on, and it was like the water clashed onto
the rock and swiped ash into dust.
As I, the dust, raised myself alone,
I was left with humbleness, which left trademarks of my parents
engraved on my heart.

As I got close to edge of the water,
I gazed at the reflection:
Surprised, amazed, and astonished.

No, I couldn't believe my eyes.
How could have I raised myself into this?
It was like I've never seen anything so beautiful as my reflection.

I thought something went wrong in the chromosomes that were put together,
To make such beautiful thing last forever.
I screamed out, "Am I the moon? Are you being for real?"

So I looked up to try spot the moon because I couldn't believe my eyes anymore.
It was dark and cloudy.
I couldn't find it, but in fact it was a hidden surprise.
It was a hidden surprise blocked from my sight.
I was the one missing from the sky.

So I chose to leave this earth to shine on others.
I wanted to be an inspiration for all these youngsters.
Feeling like I didn't belong here from the beginning,
But indeed I was put on earth to show some meaning.

There is a reason for every human living.
Don't you ever think that your life has no meaning.
Because once you are asked to define your life,
And you look back at those times,
Different shades and glimpses appear with different types of smiles.

2
A smile that is paid for never has the same effect as a smile that was intentionally planted on your beautiful face.
I learnt that it shows more meaning when it's mixed with real feelings and emotions.

In fact, don't leave anyone or anything that has a purpose for your intoxicated smile.
They are the best thing anyone can wear and are contagious within a mile.
In the end,
I figured out the missing piece that made the puzzle complete.

It was the moon, who had holes on the surface of its face caused by people who were not ashamed.
And yet it still woke up every night and shined so bright,
Till the last day it survives.
May death do us apart.

These holes were the cause to my smile.
There are reasons to smile everywhere around me.
Like I said, I'm up there to inspire,
To make people look up upon me.

And if you've had enough of life,
Just look up.
The moon could be a sign
To save your life tonight.
Unwrap your dreams outside your mind.

You have a mouth for a reason,
A voice that God blessed you with for people to listen.
Stay positive, loyal, and decent.

Hold the door wide open for whoever has a bad impact on you
and your future
Close the doors after that, as the door may let a few memories in
between the space bound clearance.
After a while,
Although the memories will linger, the aftereffect will disappear,
so there will be no reason for you not to smile.

Be as bright as you can and set your dreams for as long as you
want.
Prove that you are the most beautiful person anyone could have,
even after the scars.

For you, my dear,
I'll keep you locked up in my memory.
You've left a unique scar in the middle of my heart unintentionally.

Life and Its Game of Cards

21/06/14

I sinned today differently than yesterday.
Tomorrow I'm guaranteed I'll sin in conjunction with the other days.
Life is just like a game of cards:
We don't know how it's going to start.
You can choose to win or lose; you've got the cards in between your palms.

It's a mystery you have to solve though.
The meaning comes from the way you carry yourself throughout the game.
You can always trick society with a flame that once created fame to your name.
If you get caught in that state of mind, then there is no one but you to blame.

Do we have to send society back to rehab for it to become normal again?
I'm afraid we cannot, because irreversible changes have been already made.
We just have to learn how to live with the pain that is in our brain.
I ask my peers to forgive me,
As I am human who tries to give all my love to those who are needy.

I remember them every now and then.
I'm sorry, but sometimes I forget.
It's just I've got so many things on my mind carrying me away that I regret.
I'm not mad, but I bet you don't understand,
Because you haven't been through half the things I've forcefully suffered from.
My pain attacked the pretty smile that was once on my face.
Then it left a mark saying that it will haunt me back in the dark.

When I try to count my sins, I end up losing the plot.
I cry with my eyes wide open so that I don't get caught in my own thoughts
And after that, I end up figuring out which sin led to the beginning of all this.
Let's be honest:
If I hadn't committed that sin the other day,
I wouldn't have learnt from my mistake.

I will own up to the things I know I have done wrong.
But who the hell are you to tell me that you're a judge?
Can you remind me of the last time you did something to help the world?
Instead, you tie your tongue to your ears and hold a grudge.

I guess you're full of nothing, but you're deceitfully trying to believe your own lies.
Now, things like this get to me, because the day I die,
You're all going forget the things I sacrificed.
I held your tear up when you were about to cry,
Just to turn your sorrows into a voice in disguise.

The first time I sent my sacrifice away, it was from the bottom of my heart.
This time it's from the butterfly that was created by pure love.
Tomorrow we shall see if I wake up to be the same dreaming person I have always been,
To conquer the reasons behind all my sins.

Torn Apart

01/07/14

1

After years of hardship, my only brother got asked what he was missing out on the most.
I'll never forget the words I heard, which broke me again, leaving the feeling of a stroke.
As he was lying down on the bed, he turned around and whispered to me instead.

"I'm missing Mummy and Daddy's love.
A choice has been made that I am forced to accept.
I don't want to be caught in the money game.
I'm human not a property that's held for rent."

I became speechless at the time. My heart was filled with regret.
If only I knew how to play the role of being Mummy and Daddy instead,
I could have been his heart saver.
As he was sleeping, I heard a voice coming from him again.
"I miss you … I miss you."

Then I began to question myself. Who was there to heal his mess?
He is torn apart with different heartaches and is pleading for attention.
I'm sick and tired of having to raise my voice over his, but again I'm trying to discipline him because I'm playing Mummy and Daddy till God knows when.

He has no clue about my intentions and actions toward his mentality.
I've always loved to show love to him, but it always backfired at me because it wasn't me whom he needed.
Even though he pleaded for attention, it was toward a certain thing,
For Mum and Dad's love and caring.

2

Mum raised me up saying if anything happens in the future, I should take her role for my brother.
I nodded my head even though I thought there was no point in taking it seriously.

I'm all grown-up now. Things did drift away.
Now after things changed, it was forced upon my soul to look after my brother.
I wanted him to grow up knowing the meaning of life and its consequences, but at the same time I didn't want him to grow faster than what he was supposed to.

Memories that were restricted, unforgettable, and undeniable have been the cause to everything that has led to this moment.
As the older one, I took most of the past sorrows so that it wouldn't affect him as much.

Her Unique Personality

01/7/14

I have a strange personality that keeps me focused.
You will you never hear my pains because usually they're covered
by my smile, unspoken about.
But I've always loved to translate my thoughts into words and
compose them into poems.

They're stories that define my life and true experiences,
To show people that there is another person out there who might
be going through the same but different struggles,
And therefore give them no reason to fall into clearance.

I love to keep myself distant
Because I'm very different.
Sometimes people's opinions get to me, and all of a sudden I feel
so strange.
I don't know why the people in this world have taken me so
seriously.

Is it because of my appearance?
Is it because I'm an easy target?
Or is it because of my different spirit?

It's like a game of brilliance.
Everyone has kept their distance.
I know I've reached my limit
Because as my lips ache, they turn violet.

The Backstabber

05/08/14

I try to go to school with a positive thought in my head,
But that is the place where I get hurt the most, I swear.
It taught me that there will always be haters who smile in your
face,
Or hug you tight, begging for you to stay,
Then later on go online and get carried away.

They sit behind the screen acting all tough and say
Words that they swore they'd never phase
It's a repeated routine they use and try to downplay
Every single sneaky move they do behind your back till this day.

They try to portray a cool image about themselves,
Thinking there is no damage done toward the innocent ones who
seek for help.
In reality it's like they've set the gun free, aiming at their hearts
and minds.
Meanwhile, they were brought onto this earth so fragile.

Do the cool ones even know how it feels to be left out?
No.
And that's a problem because they have no sympathy, and
therefore they carry on.
Did they admit that they teased me, or did they say it was just a
few words to carry out a laugh?

I'm sure they're in need of a heart after hurting me and saying
that it was just all a joke.
I will laugh along with them sometimes to show that it didn't get
to me,
Because really it shouldn't.

But I never asked for any sort of damage to begin with.
It dug a huge hole in the membrane of my heart while I was trying to take it easy.
I won't lie—it's a divine move to make
When you act tough and care about others while being stepped on, and downplayed.

The Witness

19/08/14

A little girl had the camera faced straight at her,
Talking about how the Israel solders bombed the country she was
born and raised in, to try to conquer
The land that Gaza owns
By exceeding the boundary zone.

They sent solders and many drones
To burn people and turn humans back into bones.
Within the volume of our television, you can hear all the groans
That are developing from the innocent ones who don't have a
clue; they just don't know,
And the only choice they have is to go on with the flow.

It's sad that these innocent people have to go through things that
have nothing to do with them.
The girl shed tears, saying her age was ten,
And that she was forced to witness her grandmother and uncle
turn back into ash again.
May our prayers be heard and accepted.
Amen.

Groups of Israelis laugh at each bomb that explodes as if it's a
show hosted by a comedian.
Can someone please explain to these innocent people how
humanity neglected them?
They cry to the camera and camera men;
Then their voices are unheard and their tears are unseen because
media has covered up on the so-called businessmen.

They're people who get paid to take away people's lives.
What happened to everyone having their own God damn rights?
These innocent people don't get to sleep from fright.
Muslim ladies covered up from head to toe during day and night.

A powerful bright light shooting out of their faces, forcing us to cover our eyes,
Explaining it all, making us realise
That they don't deserve to have their lives taken. Because as one by one die,
This earth shines less,
And therefore that has created holes in the middle of our chests.
May we raise our hands and ask for the best!
They're full of shame and yet no regret.
When it comes to all seriousness, it is our voices they're in need,
To make sure another child does not bleed.

It's Spelt Moon with a Capital B

25/08/14

1
A bitterly cold night on the beach, alone.
There was something unusual about the sky today, which wasn't always shown.
Something that rarely happens, but when it does,
It's a memory that can only be captured with an eye stone.

Clouds were booming out with condensed vapour water,
But that wasn't the strange thing about this night.
A vibrant-coloured, natural satellite that caught my eyes right away.
It stole my breath just like when a kidnapper steals a child from its parents while walking on a pathway.

His scent was vein strong.
I craved him since that day.
It was time to settle down near this beautiful beach after what the moon had shown me straight away.

The way it was looking down on me made me who I am today:
Humble with a bit of imperfection mixed with clay.
The colour of the sky was covered with angry clouds, and what was left shining is white and grey.

I didn't understand why the clouds acted in such a way, because I hadn't felt this kind of pain in days.
Did the moon hire bodyguards to cover its dais?
But you already have muscles that take the place of two metal armours.

I couldn't tell the difference between the bullet and a nasty flame.
Didn't it want me to stay?
You can say all you want, but we both know I pleaded for this stage.
Please don't let something so beautiful end with dismay.

But it's the moon I needed.
I went from someone falling into a hole full of troubles to someone who is aware of what needs to be heeded.
I was never perfect, but I guess you looked at me different.

2
I drowned you with respect, so how can you neglect the love I had for you?
My soul was ceded,
And my emotions were controlled with a pile of coal.
You took me as a whole and then returned me to the buttonhole.

It affected me as much as how poetry affects society,
Because it's a bunch of words put together that not just anyone knew how to combine.
Who are you fooling? The blind?
If you're reading this and you're still seated without any hesitation,
Then I guess this nation deserves to be told what you did to me—no questioning needed.

I loved and still love you anyway.
Can we start all over?
Can you demand those clouds to uncover your beauty all over again?
I can't handle your aroma.
I hardly remember things, but I remember exactly the last time I woke up from a coma.

Instead of them injecting me with words I didn't want to hear,
Couldn't I have had a kiss to save me from this?

I screamed out your name the other night.
Did you hear it, or was it astray from your eyesight?

My Imagination

01/09/14

1
I fell deep into something imaginary.
All the imaginational stories I created of you and me in the back
of my head needed a dictionary
To define my thoughts,
To define my feelings,
To define what made me so full of grief.

Who was there to help me through my disbelief?
Nobody.
Not even the bloody thief who stole my heart within a few hours.
I stood on top of a high reef,
Wanting to end my life because I could barely breathe,
Thinking that if I was to take my life away it will be a relief.
But the truth was
I wasn't going to be in a better place.

I was going to be six feet down where the deadliness lays and the
mysterious adventure leads.
It's like a waste of all my good deeds failing to be seen.
People saw me bleeding with tears of harshness,
But not one asked me if I was okay.

2
See, now, that's the problem with acting all strong and happy in
front of people all the time.
They think it's only been going on for a while and that you'll get
over it after you walk a mile.
But really, it's a lifestyle.

A style of life you live in when you are unable to answer the question to why you are still alive.
They can't see what you see.
They can't feel what you feel.
And most of all, they cannot compare what you're going through with their journeys, because no matter how much they say they know how your pain feels,
Truth is,
They have no clue.

I knew if I didn't react straight away to how I felt,
Then I was going to get worse.
It's about time I take action.
I started off with baby steps to get out of this.
And now I'm ready to face the beginning of my new journey with bliss.

Endless Thoughts after What I Had Been Taught

07/09/14

The land owners have been distinct,
Only because they had different beliefs.

No sorry was given until a few years ago,
Because the newest owners of this land had them at their
demand down below.

New flags with new colours,
Ruling the land of others.

They signed papers with the blood of innocent people
And stamped its approval with tears that you'll only see when you
look straight into their pupils.

It was a tradition to throw the boomerang far away and expect it
to come right away,
But after the land was taken over,
They gave it a makeover.
And it's sad when you look right over to your shoulder
To find more people being diagnosed with racist vocabularies,
which are undefined in dictionaries.

It was white or attack;
Now it's white and black.

Because laws have been made after we treated them with
disgrace.
We didn't count the true land owners as humans because they
were different in colour.
The tone of their skin used as an excuse, controlling us dollar by
dollar.

And we are not aware of their broken hearts.
It all started with thieves.
Thieves were claimed to be role models,
The cause of stolen generation after generation.

Meanwhile, they introduced rabbits to create fusion with kangaroos,
And fed them more than the children they stole, so that we can watch the pests grow and the mistreated humans downgrade way below with mild abuse.

The shining stars of the land have turned dull after being attacked with arrows and swords
Hungry for pieces from the land surrounded by shores.

I wonder how they stepped a foot onto the land.

Perhaps they were ships unsinkable, able to travel long distances to get a strand of land by putting their hands on a property that isn't theirs and naming it with a new, known brand.

But I believe it was all planned.

A command to change what once was called Greenland to Motherland, owned by the commonwealth and designed by royals to get a new generation to expand.
Let's wake up ourselves.
Let's acknowledge how this land was and still is owned by the people of the boomerang.

Lesson after Lesson

30/09/14

If I stole your heart, would you accept the fact that I won't give it back? Because when I love, I love hard; when I smile, I smile hard; and when I cry, I cry hard. I have no in-betweens. I couldn't care less if I didn't fit into society no more. I learnt it the hard way. I mean, sometimes I can't even love myself from how much hurt I've endured.

I might come across as the most stuck-up bitch or some annoying girl. And that just proves to me that no one actually knew who I was. Nobody wanted me to be who I really was. They wanted me to act as they please. But I was a girl lost in her dreams, so caught up with things I couldn't even turn my dreams into reality. In my mind I had never thought love could be from one side until the age of a teen. At that age I met someone. In my eyes he was so beautiful; words couldn't describe him. I was left with no choice but to classify him as the moon, the one and only. From then on, nothing was the same. To the world he looked like just another guy, but in my eyes he looked so different to every other guy. He was my ideal man back then.

I am a year older at this very moment, and I have been battling with my heart for an ongoing twelve months. To this day I don't know how long it's going to take for me to win my heart over this mess. A chaos. High on love, leaving me blunt. I've become so mysterious. It was out of my control. I couldn't control the way I felt toward certain people, and this is the reason why I feel like I'm dying slowly. Each and every day, I counted the stars till I fell asleep. I'd lose count as I fell into a steep dream that has been haunting my vision ever since I can't remember when.

Why am I still in love with something I can't have? I've reached out to the moon many times before, but there was a long amount of distance hovering above me. I had to accept the fact that if the moon wanted me, he would at least try to notice my hand

held right up in the air. He didn't. In fact, he didn't even notice I existed at all. Someone else existed in his mind, and that wasn't me. Yeah, it's sad that I have become such a silly person, thinking that one day I will win his heart. I won't. I never will.
Dedicated to my old self.

Another year from then. I realised everything in him wasn't what I needed. I needed a man. He looked manly, yet he was just a boy. I admit that I was blind. Blind enough to not see the real him. Looks can be deceiving.
I am happy it didn't end the way I thought I wanted it to be. I am even happier that it ended the way my Lord planned it to.

Chandeliers and Doubt in Sanity

14/10/14

I lost my mind trying to read his.
What have I lead myself to?
Been holding for so long onto a chandelier,
Expecting it to lift me high above gravity.
But instead I have fallen hard into cavity.

The depravity leaves me confused.
I'm used to being so used and abused that I have refused to take
the word *sorry* as the healer for my bruise.

That word has done nothing as I feel the need to steal an
apology.
I'm only very sensitive when it comes to being lied to or
mistreated.
An ongoing journey he left uncompleted.

I know I deserve a better chandelier,
One that will pump out strength with sincere,
Leaving my spirit ongoing and wiping all my tears.

After I witnessed the way the chandelier let me down,
My eyes hurt from seeing such an awful thing with my own vision.
Everyone else had already seen it but me.

Then later on, after a matter of trial and error, I knew if I moved
onto another chandelier for good,
I'd get credited with a crown of honour
Because I would have had found appreciation within it.

I lost hope in the chandelier that I was holding onto for so long,
Only to find a better chandelier who will support me lifelong,
Through all our rights and wrongs,
We shall remain tough and strong.

Dried Lips and Blurry Eyes

10/11/14

1

It was your name written on my dried lips with the same venom
you constantly spilt in my eyes.
I burnt myself up to give you light,
Just like a candle filled with fright.
I had become nothing but soulless after that.
I have lost my soul trying to find yours.
My love for you was vein strong,
Not until I found out that I had escaped your fancy memory.

I turned into something I wasn't just yesterday,
Because I was traumatised by the way you hurt me after
acknowledging how much you loved me.
After that, I thought I didn't ever want to hear a lie,
But from you the lie came out so truthfully.
My ears had mistaken the sound of your warm tone
approaching me.

From you I accepted every nothing you gave me because I had
fallen for your drowsy eyes.
I always seemed to be hopeless, but I still never hoped less.
That's why I kept the chances coming.
After the third chance,
I should have known you weren't going to change.

I remember as a nine-year-old, I would carry my little Razor scooter,
And when it would hit my ankle, it'd leave me feeling like the
world was collapsing.
I am sixteen, and every time I held you high,
You would aim right for my heart with a bow and arrow made out
of fire.
I woke up from denial to find out you had me cursed under your
childish love after presenting yourself as a man on character
parade.

Love No More

15/11/14

I told you look at my bare skin,
Uncolour my eyelashes, and gloss my lips with one last kiss.
Say something sweet to make my rosy cheeks peak.
But you refused to look at me.
You didn't even try to wipe my black tears.
Instead, you suffocated me by covering my mouth, and you told
me I was no longer the one you need.

Maid of Honour

19/11/14

When you are around me, my heart would begin to skip a beat.
I wore no makeup in your presence.
I began not to care about the regrowth of my hair because I
knew my natural colour was priceless.
Only, did I ever want all my skin to be exposed in front of you, in
case I was to get lost?
You'd find me alive in my dead skin.
I claimed my face as a canvas and called it a piece of art.
I've been covering my pale face with a coat of white paint called
make-up ever since you weren't near.
Separating lash from lash with a brush covered in black to make
them look long and thick.

Insecurities held me back from heaps of things,
But the Lord sent you my love to unwrap me.
And finally I witness the sun sending its glory through its shine.
Now I'm known as the maid of honour.

The Wise Believer

28/11/14

If I exposed to you my tears of joy,
If I allowed you to access what my life really feels like,
Of which will you believe?
Of which will overpower the other?

I'm Junkie Love for You

29/11/14

I threw up your name last night, and it felt just like the
Way a junkie would react to a hangover.
Also,
I spilled you out of my mind,
Just like a junkie would tip his leftover.

Junkies don't get hangovers;
Nor do they deal with drinks.
They overdose on love.

In other words, I kept quiet,
Silent,
Bullet strong,
Naive.

Show vs. Reality

01/12/14

Skin deep her beauty laid.
Mind in,
Her attitude needed to be covered by a Band-Aid.

Silence is not an answer

01/12/14

Stop downplaying how you feel toward me.
Bipolar could only describe you mostly.
After all the silent hours we heard together,
All the hissing snakes in you had a get-together,
Tongue tied,
Changing colour from time to time.

The Silent Affection

01/12/14

Silent feelings affected me like a silent gun would affect anyone.
You were almost half here,
And figuring you out was deadly.

Mockingbird

02/12/14

Pain mocked,
Tears struck,
Attention earned.
Yet,
Not from the right one.

Fake Smiles

02/12/14

No more real smiles.
Eyes filled with tears.
Empty hearted,
Held back by fears.

Sacrificing a lifetime for people who wouldn't take a look back to
see what's up.

The Wise Diver

06/12/14

When you looked her straight in the eye,
It felt like you dived a thousand miles into the blue sea.
When your ears heard the way she spoke,
You accepted and devoted more time to find her lost tear.
Without fear you sacrificed thousands of miles to figure out what
she hadn't shown you
She didn't show you everything at the start,
So you dedicated your commitment to detach the grip of a hard
rock from the bottom of her shell,
Just for another peek to discover the beauty within her art.

What Is Love?

08/12/14

I was asked to define the meaning of love.
Although I couldn't answer it with words,
I took your hand and placed it on my chest.
It was the letters of your name wrapped around my heart.
Nothing was fonder than the memories that occurred afterward.
The sentence "I love you" never did much for me,
As it was actions that spoke louder than words.
The warm texture revolving around us after hugging each other
so tightly made me feel like the safest girl in the world.
When I felt the world go against me,
You lifted me up to the highest level possible,
Just so I could see that there is more to life than I ever thought
there was.
If I was to cross the street without looking left or right,
You'd be my saviour.
When someone speaks of you,
The word *hero* comes to mind.
You saved me from a wave that had me suffering unbearable
pain.
No word could describe the meaning of love.
A reminder from you to smile etched in the voice of my head;
Hence it was the only reason to why I am able to walk another
mile.
Though I'm still fragile,
You are the glue gun to all my broken piles.

Quality

09/12/14

Gym is a place of imperfection.
Big, small, thick, and thin.
Short, tall.
Where do I begin?
Those individuals are no different to the others just because of the
size of their skin.
This place I speak of is the start to a new healthy lifestyle,
From girls and boys to ladies and gentlemen giving it all
they've got
To create more strength within all the time they fought,
Creating a new routine.
And for a better figure, they start a strict regime.

Now, here's the thing.
Not everyone is on the same level.
So if you see yourself doing better than others,
Be humble.
There's no need to have pride in what you achieved.
Be happy and let your new character have an effect on others'
dreams.
Motivate them with all the knowledge they haven't yet seen.
Your success will surely help others conquer their dreams.
Let the results push you to help others that are in need.
You are just like everyone else.
You started from the bottom; now you're here.

The Heavens' Servant

10/12/14

O Mother, O Mother, O Mother,
I am sorry for all the pain I caused you.
When I was much younger, I brought out your flaws.
Because of all the sick days I was diagnosed with,
You laid there suffering with me.
Your heart aches in the middle of my harsh cough,
And also when the fever running through my body won't cool off.
My tears had you wide awake throughout the night
And I never knew this until I grew up and it was too late.
I said to myself that I wouldn't have been here till this day
If it wasn't for you, who helped me fight my sickness away.
Some days I talk louder than my limit.
I'm sorry, Mother. I do pray day and night to be forgiven.
You are not only my mother.
You are my friend, sister, and listener.
My heart is attached to yours.
The heavens lie under your feet.
I have no right to treat you like this.

You're mistreated.
I love you and forever will love you.
Without you, I'm incomplete.

Unexplainable

13/12/14

You are the dearest, my love.
You are the closure of my heart when the shadow of my body escapes.
You leave me with words I cannot yet start to explain.
I took you by surprise.
Now you're the only thing I could name.

Won't you tell me what page?

13/12/14

Although you were visible,
The love you served was invisible.
I didn't know what page you were on, on most days.
I flicked through your entire book to find something worth reading.
You left me with no choice but to tear it into more than one piece.

Your Childish Love and Sickness

13/12/14

In the back of my mind, I was fed up with your sick excuses,
But at the bottom of my heart, my heartbeats couldn't stop
creating excuses for you.
They said that the heart wants what it wants,
But I knew if I was to follow my heart,
I'd fall into another trap of his.
So instantly I left.
I left everything that meant the world to me behind.
Lost for comfort,
Found in dust.

Unplanned Murder

13/12/14

I was his hero;
He was mine.
We were two kids lost in time.

Time past;
He was gone.
She was crying to him on his tombstone.

The baby kicked back and forth in her tummy.
Yielding for a life on this earth.
However, he was still far too young to be produced,
So she swallowed down a pill.
Never in her life did she plan someone to kill.

The Withdrawer

15/12/14

The utterance that withdrew out of his mouth was found guilty.
He killed a soul unintentionally,
Thinking the muscle of his tongue wouldn't be as powerful.

But in fact he was so wrong.
The tongue was throne strong.
It occurred that the tongue was put high up in a place where it does not belong.
It was now time to play a ritual song.
Bing, bang, bong.

Nothing Could Compare

15/12/14

After all the songs and stories written about love,
No tune could blossom into the reality of life.
There will always be a hidden love story,
Or a truth behind a mankind's emotion.

No words could compare,
However thoughts will sink deep in despair.

Unsensational

The main thing that triggered my heartbreak was because I was emotional. However, he was senseless.

Of Which Is Home?

19/12/14

His arms felt like home more than anything else.
At least I didn't have to pay for that.

We exchanged our feelings regardless of how emotionally
drained we were.
And I can swear by anything that I could never feel as safe when
he is far from reach.
If I was to complain about my house not feeling like home, would I
get a refund?
If I were to complain about his arms not feeling as safe anymore,
what would be my only solution?
The grounds of both the heavens and hellfire will shake rapidly
with agony until I reclaim my words.
"Do not underestimate the power of being safe and sound," they
told me.

An Unseen Repenter

12/12/14

I've sinned so many times,
And in conjunction with the tears of regret, they were combined
To produce a sea,
A sea full of sins named by the queen.
It was forever remembered as Sin Shell.
But nobody knew that those sins I committed were also the ones
that I repented over.
It was supposed to be between me and the Lord,
Yet people had already caused damage.
They mouth every situation into their own scenario.
And now all that's known about Sin Shell are rumours.
But I knew that to God, Sin Shell was one of the most pure water
anyone could touch.
So I laid back into happiness, and all I felt was God's angels take
this soul of mine.

Their Talk Is so Cheap

22/12/14

I sit here lost in wonder.
Also, I try to see why
These people I trusted are composing so many lies about me.
The thought of it sickens me, so I'm left with no choice but to
ignore it.
The feeling won't go away,
And the more silent I am,
The more they create their own scenario to portray.
Am I paranoid?
I must be reading things so wrong.
Though they knew one percent about me,
They still talked cheap for so long.
If I'm not the one feeding it, then who is? Won't you tell me what's
going on?
I hear screaming and yelling all about what I did wrong.
You expect a phone call from me to lie and defend you—also to
give you so much attention to please your needs.
These actions are false now.
Also, all the mixed signals you send need to be controlled.
I'm all grown up, not here to play pretend.
As I sit here and wonder about the reason for all your hate,
I realise that you don't deserve my energy; there's no time in the
world for me to waste.
Relationship's broken after being in touch for so long.
She is all that mattered.
Why was that so wrong?
You can hate me if hatred against your brother brings a good
deed to wipe away your sin.
But I don't understand why you feel the need to toss tales within.
Are you content in the lie you live?

Underestimation of the Unknown

23/12/14

Just because you don't cry,
That does not mean you aren't sad.
Just because you don't cut,
That does not mean you aren't hurting from the inside.
Remember: an individual's therapy may vary depending on how strong one is,
Or how one has been raised by society.
Because when I'm sad and hurt,
All my mind starts thinking is pen and paper.
So for me, drawing and writing will be my only answer.
The difference between you and me
Is that I draw with a sharp pencil, but you draw with a sharp razor and claim it's art.
"Why don't we discover each other's side of art by exchanging our sharp equipments?" I asked desirably.
The aftermath was the only answer to that question.
The one who used to cut herself skin deep became an artist that draws the brightest side of life.
However, the one who used to draw her spirit on a piece of paper with a sharp pencil
Fell into misery and ended her life with the same clean cut razor used before her.
Do not underestimate an individual's sadness.
And mostly,
Do not underestimate what one's equipment is capable of composing.
You will regret it.

Woman of Modesty

24/12/14

"O woman of modesty, who are you trying to please?" they
asked me
Not the creation, my dear.
"Then who?"
The creator.

The Poisonous Potion

24/12/14

Don't smile in my face and expect me not to smile back.
Don't hurt me and expect me to be okay with that.

I'm just as human as you.

The difference between you and me is the way we advertise our emotions.
Maybe it was planned that you are to be born with a smile that could confuse people.
Or perhaps the creator unintentionally misspelt the spell, and you were what came to conclusion.

The taste of your potion was poisonous.
But damn, it was hella addictive.

What Is He Falling For?

24/12/14

He grieved to me with agony, "Why won't you let me love you?"
"Because you will fall," I replied with dismay.
"I have already fallen for you," he acknowledged while placing
my hands in his.

But he didn't understand that if I let him in,
If I let him walk around in my heart,
He wouldn't be falling for me—rather, he would be falling into
holes.

"What are those holes you speak of?" people asked me.

Before I got to my answer,
"How does it feel to drive on a road that is permeated with
potholes?" I asked rhetorically.
Because going for a walk in my heart will feel the exact
same way.
The holes there formed from people who entered and then left
without sympathy, causing wounds.

Thank the Lunar

25/12/15

Growing up, I was bullied into silence.
Who helped me find the way to guidance?
Who coached me out of shyness?

It was the moon,
And I was the client.
I didn't turn to smoke, drugs, or violence
Because I remember that the moon taught me to do better than
that.
Indeed, it also taught me how to shine even on my darkest nights.

However, I asked about why my misery ached the most in the dim
of every light.
When the day came to end,
The moon shined,
And all I saw was the darkest colours beaming outside from its
own cavities.
From then I knew that it only happens to beautiful things.

The moon was my only listener, my motivator, and most of all
It was my number one supporter.

The Way Society Works

28/12/14

Hi.
My name is society, and I would like to preach out to you and say,
Be yourself!
Embrace your talents!
Laugh as much as you want!
Dress not to impress!
Be with whomever you feel like being with!

But no. Not like that.

Hello there, again.
Remember, I am society, and I will constantly be watching over and judging you.
Because I'm made of different genders, beliefs, cultures, and backgrounds.

So if weird is what defines you, I will look at you as if you aren't cool.
If you go a day without wearing make-up,
"She thinks she looks good" are words that come straight to mind.
If he didn't have time to cut his hair, he is dirty.
If you laugh over and over a joke after it died out, I will look at you as if you lack maturity.
If you have the most beautiful voice, I will tell you that you don't, just because I can't hear you sound better than me.
If you enjoy playing sports, to me you think you are the best player.
If you run desirably toward the swings at the park just to blow the mess off your chest, you are acting like a child.
If you cover up all your hair and body, I will oppress you.
If you wear tight jeans, it will automatically appear to me that you are an attention seeker.
If you are with the guy I was having trouble getting with, then guess what?
You are a man stealer.

If I wasn't able to get the attention I wanted from your girl, she is stuck up.

My name is society, and you are welcomed (not by choice) to the most bittersweet of it all.

Now deal with it.

Sincerely, the society we live in.

Voiceless

While I was craving the whole you,
You craved one thing.
You showed me it by planting a kiss on my lips,
Only because that was the thing you most missed.
You went days without wanting to speak to me,
And all I ever wanted you to do was listen.
I had no friends to share my feelings with.
My vocabulary filled up more and more words each day,
So I suffocated within the struggle to keep my voice locked in.
My mouth has become voiceless,
But I have eyes and a smile that could speak louder than words
ever will.

Don't Lay Your Hands on Me

30/12/14

Why do you call it frigid when I say don't lay your hands on me, unless strings are attached?
I get told I'm frigid all the time; there is something they don't understand
It's that I don't feel comfortable when any guy touches me. I think it's totally irrelevant, and if they feel the need to express what they want, they can speak it.

Are we not taught enough to take care of ourselves?
Are we not ordered to respect our morals?
Because if you ask any guy,
He would want his wife to be clean.
But for you to be that, you must know what they are worth, my dear.
So please, ladies, when I tell you stay away from men who are immature when it comes to relationships,
It's only because the day a man asks for your hand, people will have nothing to speak bad of you.
Rather, your parents will raise their heads high proud of you.
They say what you are, you get.
Be the best so that you can get it in return.
And may the creation find you the best spouse who is suitable for you.

The Tip of His Fingers Were Needle like

31/12/14

The tip of your fingers were needlelike
When I went to hold your hand.
It felt just like grabbing onto a stem full of thorns after being fooled
by how beautiful the rose looked.
I knew reaching out for the stem means getting cut.
I was also warned about not touching sharp things with my bare
hands.
And even though I knew that you didn't want my hands
anywhere nearby,
I still wanted to keep in touch.
I was so rebellious I couldn't resist my hands not being in yours.
So I gave you no choice, and in return you raged at me with the
deepest voice of all.
From then I was frightened.
Frightened to even rethink what we had was a thing.
I deserved more than just your lust; I guess I didn't know what I
was worth at the beginning,
So I let your ego take control of me.
And now you have me tied under a unreversed curse.
My heart is polluted by your breath.
I need to get sent back to rehab.
Why won't someone take a walk in my shoes?
Guaranteed you won't cope a few steps, from all the blisters it
creates.
And because I gave you my all,
I'm filled with pins and needles. Also, one thing eats me up at
night all the time.
It's the feeling of regret and fright.

Torture

31/12/14

Sometimes I overdose on overthinking; my mind begins to freeze.

Other times no thoughts appear due to the ache caused by how harsh people can be to me.

Don't control me to suit the way you feel today.
I might not be feeling you at all, and that's a shame.
It's like torture.

The Mask

31/12/14

His commitment and my commitment weren't the same.
That's why we didn't last.

Although what was shown on his face was filled with sparks,
I later on realised he was wearing a mask.

Fancy

1/1/15

He was one of the most things I fantasised.
What did I even fancy about him, though?
Was it the way his smile lit every dull part of me?
Was it his beard that shaped perfectly on point?
Or was it the sense of humour he let out when I had nothing to
laugh about?

Perhaps it was everything about him.
But is he a man of his words?

The answer is where the future holds.

Bittersweet

03/1/15

You stare insanely into a photo that you've captured years ago,
trying to understand what distinguishes between the one you
took recently and the ones you took before.

The faces have changed.
Less people in the background,
Which means the people you socialised with are no longer the
same.

People who didn't even risk walking a few steps for you managed
to overpower you.
Oh, all the puddles you jumped for people who did you wrong.
But you're all grown up now,
And your soul doesn't tick with many humans any more.
But I knew.
I knew for a matter of fact that the bodies around me now would
take on any challenge that is held against me, holding a sword
and ready for attack.

Through memories that were bittersweet, I learnt that not many
people were willing to grow old with you.
Hands down, an image can speak so much louder than words.

Do Me Right

03/01/15

Shower me with your time.
Water my potential with your support.
Lead me to your arms.
When I have wronged each footstep to cut my life short,
As I suck your love dry,
Promise me you will bring more sunshine to my life.

Quality Time

04/01/15

I never asked for heels, bags, or diamonds from you.
I can support myself with all that whenever I feel like it.

Rather, I ask you to find time for me
In your busy life.

Day vs. Night

05/01/15

Do you ever wonder
Why those tears that drop down your face at 2:00 a.m. feel more damaging than ever?
When you try to compare it to your 2:00 p.m. cry, somehow the meaning of each am tear will overpower the other.

If I were to scream out my all,
I will choose the day.
You know why?
Because the voice at night sounds louder and will travel further to the unknown,
And I don't want that to happen.
I don't want the unknown to be aware of my hopeless nights.

The day is aware that I take advantage of it,
And the pitch-black dark will always be a witness to every reason why I shred another scar.

Her Faith

06/01/15

Her beauty was unforgettable.
Speaking about how well-known she was for doing the things she
enjoyed most,
Her talent boosted far away into success,
Honoured for being a woman with respect.

But when he met her,
It wasn't just how successful she was that attracted him.
It was the way her scarf covered her up.
It pointed out that there is more strength within her beauty than
what is already shown.
He knew then what was hidden from the world will only be
exposed to his eyes.

Forever the humbleness in her heart will grow.

Love Is Lost

06/01/15

Is it my fault that the love I crave is lost?
It's lost in you.
I don't control the way my eyes light up when you're in my presence.
I can't control the way my heart beats when I'm thinking of you.

You don't understand how much I crave the feeling of you being around, and that's something I can't control either.
You're the only answer to all my wishes.

A day will come were you'll feel like something is missing in you.
And till that day comes,
I'll be hopelessly waiting for you to choose me
To complete you.

Out of Sight

06/01/15

You never thought I would get used to you not being around.
But as I grow up each day without you,
The thought of you grows out of my way.
I stayed out of sight, and ever since then,
You have escaped my mind.

Eye Contacts

07/01/15

Usually when I fall in love,
I am not able to look him in the eye.
And that's when I know my feelings have hit the other side of his heart.
He who managed to steal my eyesight
Has no idea though.

Later on, after I got caught up in my feelings,
It was time I faced my fears and proved to myself that I was capable of all this.

When my eyes laid on the same level as his,
I began to notice a monster sitting in the middle of his pupil.
As I noticed it straight away,
I found it strange,
Because the last time I felt a connection,
I was fooled by the contacts in his eyes.

Fearless

11/01/15

Getting taken advantage of tired her.
It was painful.
A bruise marked her life.

It was time she stopped doubting herself and finally overcome her
fears.
The actions that lead afterward were from the unpaid lessons she
got thrown at.

A thick coat of black winged eyeliner is what she drew on top of
her eyes.
Covering up her lips with blood red lipstick,
She took advantage of her bronzer and contoured her cheek
bones so dark,
Put on a serious look,
And walked out with attitude.

All that for what?

Her plan was to look fearless and unapproachable,
Just so no one could get the best of her again.

The Fragile Seed

12/01/15

No words could sugar-coat the way she felt.
After her parents divorced, it wasn't as easy as she thought it
would be.
It wasn't when things got brighter automatically.
It was like planting one seed and expecting the result of two.

How could you depend on something so small to grow without
watering it?
She was caught in between the roots of both ends,
Not knowing which end to choose to rely on.
And just after she had been planted,
She was moved elsewhere to grow.

Are you not aware of how fragile the seed is once it's planted?
It wasn't expected to grow as healthy,
But it did.

There was something nobody could understand.
Was it a miracle, or did the seed just take in the good from
the bad?

Only so Young

15/01/15

Bold eyes,
Lonely nights.

Tears drop,
Unable to stop.

Big lips,
Small talk.

Long tongue,
Only so young.

Mixture

17/01/15

With all your best,
With all my best,
Our lives start to begin, undressed.

Undeniable

17/01/15

As soon as you walked in with a great big smile,
The brightness of your perfectly lined teeth caught my attention.
It's arched in style.

The way you smelt
That night
Lingered in the tip of my nose for hours and hours.

The way your clothes were neat and tidy—
I can't lie,
I won't lie,
It turned me on.

The Unknown Reason

17/01/15

I should have known.
Known that everything you owned
Held your pride higher than the length of a cyclone.

Still owing people big money to pay off your loan,
Although all you keep doing is recalling a postpone.

You climb up people's money tree every day to sit yourself on a
throne
Designed by stones,
Heavy in weight—yet that's something you don't own.

But don't get too carried away,
Because the higher you climb,
The harder the fall will be every time.

Old Girl

17/1/15

She was young,
Yet she acted older.

Unintentionally, she grew wise,
Faster than ever.

The Thought of Repentance

18/01/15

When I stared in the mirror,
My reflection looked happy.
At least it was able to fool my drowsy eyes, just to get myself
through another dark day.

Does the thought of repentance come to my mind at all?
I'm sure God is the most forgiving.
And for every misleading action I composed forbidding him,
There's no doubt he will be a prayer way.
Llife did a great job at sucking me in.

It was time I wake up to myself.
This is not what my religion has taught me to be.
Oh God, I am sorry.
I ask for your forgiveness and mercy
For every unrepented sin I've commit.

The Doubtful Why

18/01/15

Why? she asks.

Why is it every time I pleasure my ego, I begin to realise it is then
when I have committed a sin?

Why was it every time I walked out of place, I felt my heart race?
All of a sudden the inner me turns pitch-black,
And when it came to loving someone,
That was the hardest thing to embrace.

Deceiving Look

25/01/15

He smiled so sincerely, oh lord it looked so divine
Kindness in his eyes, he only ever knew how to spread happy vibes.

He might of been able to fool us with a great big smile, but lord knows how much scars have marked his life.

Only Human

22/05/15

She grew up being taught to look and treat everyone with respect,
No matter if it is the garbage man or the president.

No matter if the individual earns heaps on a daily basis,
Or if they earned a few extra dollars on the weekend.

We are all created from the same thing.
So how could you neglect your brother's rights?

Whether they are born in a different country, from a different mother, or live with a completely different skin colour,
We are one.
We should walk the same way as each other.

Please, brothers and sisters, raise your hands and ask for forgiveness.
We are human. We are selfish. We crave for more than we need at some points.

You can't deny that you haven't thought more highly of yourself than another.
So don't reject this. I'm preaching for your benefit.

Game of Dominoes

26/01/15

As she closed her eyes and lost her balance,
Just like the game of dominoes,
She fell for him; he fell for another.

Do we blame it on her for closing her eyes?
Or shall we blame it on the strength gravity has
When one chooses to rise?

From Him

25/01/15

If you love me, let me know.
If you need me, I'll hold you close.
Just acknowledge exactly how you feel toward me.
From there I shall take the lead.
He is the missing piece to enlighten my heart, to give it peace.

Raise It Up

26/01/15

Here's to living an unhealthy life.
I'm a poet that writes about my past experiences, using my
creativity and imagination to survive.

A lady that is currently striving toward her big dreams,
Even though there are many people who don't appreciate what
they see.

The lies and tears they put me through
Made me stronger. You don't understand how much I thank you.

My haters are my motivators,
And now I'm living a great time
Without those sick individuals.
Their mouths were full of nothing but disgraceful lies.

The Nonsense Ego

26/01/15

Feeding my ego.
Just one more last time, I say.
I knew I wasn't guaranteed that I'll wake up the next day,
But I took advantage of my soul anyway.

Feeding my ego with something that pleases me.
Regretting it afterward—but that still didn't stop me from
repeating it a few times again.

The next morning I woke up in tears,
Overdosing by feeding my ego,
Losing my mind from how much I sin.
Who is it I'm supposed to fear?

I have asked for forgiveness about this particular thing,
But after that I still committed the same sin.
The amount I've fed my ego
Is something I cannot yet begin to explain.
It's something you will never believe.

There's nothing to stop its hunger.
It demands to be fed, and it aches in starvation.

O Lord, please help me regain strength in my religion once again.
Because if not,
Then forever my ego will ask for more, and I will no longer have
the guts to remain in this forbidding life.

Artificial Kiss

29/01/15

Feed me your love
While I colour my lips from how black they have turned.
As you pass through right into my mouth,
My tongue begins to ache.

It must be the artificial sweet talking you did
Just to get with me;
It was glazed with lies, sorrows, and lust.
How could I not fall for something that looks so appealing?
This was long before I tasted a piece—
A piece that had me begging you to take away from me.

Artificial Life

01/02/15

O alluring woman,
Your face looks magical.
The way it shines to catch people's attention is unbelievable.
The way your hair changes colour depending on how much the
sun shines that summer
Brings light into my life.

As I watch you place lipstick on your black liquorice lips,
My eyes begin to witness the way you position them.
O Lord, you're so neat.
If I were to kiss your beautiful red lips,
I know for a fact that they would taste sugar sweet.

O gullible man,
I encrust my wrinkly face with a sparkly mask.
On top of my bold head, I wear a wig as an illusion to show
everyone that I have hair.
As a matter of fact, I change it every summer.

My lips turned black due to my last kiss.
I could never name the one who poisoned my mouth with lies.
What he did to get with me wasn't and will never be right.

So don't be fooled by what I choose to show you.
My look is made artificially
To suit this artificial life.

Guilty

18/01/15

The pride fond in me was the reason to why I felt higher than
everybody else.
I didn't look below to see what was going on with people who
were needy.
I was there before though.
Before I was riled into the hands of a random old rich man,
I was nothing but young, gullible, and rebellious.

I let the strings attached on his fingers take major control.
It's like the day I lent him the keys to my soul.
He stamped my body with a kiss.
All I know from then is it was me he owned.
My heart was set with boundaries.
He told me if I were to get into the car with him, he would drive
me somewhere I was unfamiliar with.
I knew it would be out of bounds.
And that, if I went, there was no way back,
No way out.

I couldn't give a damn about what I did at that time.
I just wanted to live the rich life.
Most of my decisions afterward were wrong anyway, and I was
cool with that.
I was earning big money,
Penny after penny.

When I pushed down my clothes straps,
As I sat gently onto his lap,
Those coins would double up;
They turned into notes.

I never realised that this old man took my body for granted.
It was too late.
I had already turned every light green.

Yes, I was earning heaps of money,
But was I happy with what I once called a dream?
No.
The regret haunted me every time he touched me all over again.
A nightmare I thought was once my dream.
When I stare in the mirror,
In my reflection I realise this isn't who I was supposed to be.
I am guilty for disrespecting me.

Bathing Back into Earth

3/02/15

I showed up at his house only to vent to him.
However, he walked me over to the bathroom, heart naked,
Misleading my thoughts into this—what he values.
Now I was charged with hope.
Simultaneously he contemplated me lustfully.

As an act of pleasure, I placed myself gently into his bathtub,
hoping the indisposed feeling would wash away.
However, I began to realise that I was bathing myself with lies.
Lying there, allowing every indirect good-bye to incise my life.

He turned down the light
And drifted over toward me, closely.
I felt the rapture lingering through my body
"I love you so much," he then conceded.

All I can remember since drowning is the way he thrust my body
forcefully back into the Earth.

His love murdered me.

Undividable

20/01/15

How can I divide myself,
When I am not whole to begin with?

For the game that I have been served,
I am not blessed with skills to win it.

In Mummy's house, where I claim is home,
I stare right into my brother's room.
But what use is the room without its owner?

It still looks the exact same as the last time I checked
To see if he was there.

I had déjà vu.

And I am forced to believe
That it's my fault. My brother and I don't live under the same
roof—not anymore.

Sparkles vs. a Shine

15/09/14

He fell down my heart and created a big smile.
The other day when I spoke to him, after quite a while,
He was still the same.
He was still the same old, prettyful person I've ever seen.
I mean, even though he peaks every single night,
He amazes me more daily with his bright sense of humour.
The stars sparkled around to take my attention away from him,
But there was no way a sparkle would steal my attention away
from a shine.
I have a mind full of life,
Negotiating our future lives eye to eye.
I have a soul that carries its self around like a butterfly;
If it was to get lost,
I'll find it by your side.
I had a dream about you the other night,
More like every night.
Have you ever thought about why you can't fall asleep in the dark?
Legend says when you can't sleep at night, it's because you're
awake in someone else's dream.
So instead you shine so bright to be seen.
I spoke to you in a way where everyone saw it as a scream,
A scream that was locked inside me because I wanted you to
notice me.
I was way too far, I guess.
I guess we weren't meant to be.
I wonder if I hadn't met you, how different my life would have been.
At the same time,
I would kill to have you here.
If I had the power to let you see what is good in me, then I would
hold you tight and not set you free.
You will always have a special place in my heart—and that
terrifies me.

I'm no freak,
Just someone who admires you with every heartbeat.
Would you hold my hand? I'm feeling so weak.
He let me go my own way.
He didn't hold my hand.
I cried.
He never believes what I say.
I chose him over the world, hoping it's not too late,
But I lost hope in fate.

I didn't want to go out anymore.
I felt so different around others.
When I walk in public, you can point out my face because I'm tall.
Apparently I'm "too tall for a girl," this person once said.
I hated myself even more ever since then.
I couldn't accept a compliment from anyone, because I was
scared.

What was once said has now taken control over me,
Especially the love from one side I'm suffering with at this very
moment.
It's keeping my mind awake while my eyes are closed.
If I couldn't love myself, then how could anyone else love me for
who I am?

At this very moment, I couldn't understand anything but how
unlovable I am.
I can see a clear vision of him
Loving someone else.

Don't

05/02/15

Don't say you care for me,
When we both know the reason why I have scars on the sleeves of
my arms.
Those scars are stamps of evidence that you treat me otherwise.

Stop fooling me with every ineffective touch just so that I fulfil
your ego

Do not say that you love me tonight, but forget my
name tomorrow morning

I cannot cope anymore.
Do you want me to stay or go?
Ever since I let you take control of my emotions,
I haven't been feeling the same.

Even though the roots to your heart are uncoordinated,
Driving my way through without a navigator has all of a sudden
become insufficient.

You have emptied me from all the strength I had;
I'm an empty person now
Who is filled with nothing but soul.

But not just any soul—
Your soul.
Now unfree me.

As Time Passes

I'm sure I can say that I've learnt the hard way,
Trusted nasty people after forgiving them for playing their dirty
games, only to realise that their love was not genuine.

What confusess me is they had the audacity to shoot me till I died
then walked in my funeral.

Failure of the Servant

08/02/15

Sometimes we fail to praise the Lord and expect everything to go as we please.
How can we as teenagers underestimate the power of God?
How can we as a whole underestimate the power God has put into the angel of death?

O people of knowledge, where in the Qur'an does it state that we are guaranteed to live another minute?
Even without hesitation, we have the courage to choose when we want to die,
Although we as God's servants have no say.
May we all wake up to ourselves and pray
For everything we have, and ask forgiveness for everything we have taken advantage of every other day.

Red Lipstick

11/12/15

The voice of an angel trapped in her mouth allows her to warble
all night.
The candlelight living in her eyes will lead you back home feeling
high as a kite.

Her beautiful red lips will trick you to her unstable heart,
And from then, she is able to take you on—subliminally.

And you will begin to murmur unconsciously for help.

Dear God

11/02/14

Dear God,
I am standing here on the behalf of all my mistakes,
Pleading for forgiveness, or else I will go insane.

The way I dress inappropriate, to feel so confident.
It's as if I'm walking a fashion parade.
Buying tight clothes that outline my body shape was something I maintained.

I was so caught up into fitting in. Now all I want to do is escape.
I was always aware about how wrong my choices in clothes were,
but I guess now it's time for me to behave as you say.

No human can sugar-coat my regrets. O beloved, I love and believe in you.
You will forever be in my embrace.
I have committed such nonsense sins for people's sake.
But that mentality is gone now; it's something I erased.

Truth

· ·

15/02/15

I feel trapped in between my two lives.
I don't want any.
I don't want anything.
I need to find myself.
I need to find myself a place
Far away from these two messed-up cases.

I don't want their messed-up love.
I don't want their messed-up love to hurt me anymore.

I'm fed up.
I need oxygen.
I need oxygen to breathe.

I will walk myself.
I will walk myself out of this mess.
Maybe I'm not capable.
Maybe I'm not capable to do so today,
But only the future can tell.
Only the future can tell if I'm leading myself to the right place.

Or perhaps I can be leading myself to hell.

Invisible

18/02/15

He is here, yet he can barely act upon his role.
His shadow acknowledges me more than he ever will,
And our love died years ago.

It's as if I was physically there but mentally invisible.
He was oblivious while I got subliminally out of control.

Doctor, Doctor

19/02/15

The cure of my heart is trapped in your silence.
It yields to be mended,
And it tries, striving toward the surface of life.
Yet it falls downhill into agony.

You try zilch amount of times to prevent the drowning,
And speak nothing to help this disease.

Do Not Patronize Me

20/02/15

My beauty is wrapped,
And my pride is trapped
Beneath pieces of closed-off clothes.

I fall back into humbleness
When someone tries to contemplate me into thinking about
taking off my scarf,
Because no matter how much more beautiful I look without it on,
It is something that defines me.

It defines love toward my religion
And shows how much respect I have given it.
So don't bother talking me out of it;
Do not patronize me with compliments.

Sea Deep

22/02/15

Darling, look at how far you have come
From all the sleepless nights you overcome.

You defeated all your fears and climbed unsteady mountains that
were able to shake down your tears.

And now,
Now you are standing up high,
And oh the people you have inspired.

Don't ever look back.
There's so much more to come and to look forward to.
There is sea deep amount of time to find out who you are.
This is just the beginning of a new journey, O beautiful one.

Different Types of Poets

25/02/15

It's expected to have poets who have been through major heart violations or terrible experiences in life,

Because Poets express their sorrows, happiness, love, and regrets by spilling ink onto a blank piece of paper.

That's one way they are able to let out all their unheard past, untold love stories, and hidden miseries.

Other poets cut words skin deep because that is their opinion to relief.
Split flesh and blood spilling until unconscious, and not even Band-Aids could stop the bleeding.

Drinking bottles of beer as the tears crawl out, out of control, While smoking their lives away
And hopping that they will drown in a tub filled with wine.
Perhaps they will end up drowning in their own blood.

Distance

02/03/15

When lovers are distanced from each other,
Love measures itself.
The amount of space between you and the person you are
deeply attached to begins to shake with trauma when it feels
your heartache demanding to be cured.

However, nothing can be done about this
Because she is hereabouts, yet he is far, far from reach.
Pain struck the heart of two sweet lovers,
And distance has affected areas of the unknown.

Love Cure

05/03/15

Home had a beating heart.
It was yours.

The force between us pulled me closer to your arms,
And the sound of your aching soul hurt my ears.

My head is on your chest.
What a coincidence. Who knew my love for you was the only
medicine?

Walkers of the Heart

08/03/15

I'll take a walk in your heart, and perhaps you could take a walk
in mine.
We can guide each other out of shyness without a navigator,
using no incline.
You will meet the silly me, and there will be no reason for you to
refine,
To refine reasons out of my feelings for comfort.
I won't comfort you with a lie,
Because as long as you are committed,
So am I.

Sunshine and the Sandy Beach

09/03/15

Let's take a walk on the sandy beach, under the sunshine.
There is no need to worry about him or her;
Just let the remote of love take control of both our minds.
I'll be looking at your eyes, and you'll be looking straight through
into mine.

And they will ask you,
"O optimistic soldier, what do you see?"
"A fragile heart locked in the cage of sadness that needs to be
set free, out of madness."

Harness Me to the Sun

12/03/15

I rambled my way down the midst of a pitch-black road.
I saw nothing but sadness with these dark eyes of mine though.
My tears—
They drained all the energy kept in both eyes,
Sealed lids.
Candles build, and they grow inside.

The moment I tried to open these drowsy eyes,
Then is when I felt the world collide and ignite.
And if the only way to brighten up is by harnessing myself to
the sun.
I will burn my skin to shower my eyes out of fright.

O Moon, O Moon, O Moon

13/3/15

O vibrant mind-boggling Moon,
I'm sorry that some people don't notice you.
You wait for so long to shine at night,
Yet they don't take the chance to look up at you.

O impaired Moon,
When people don't try to understand your language,
I am the one to talk you out of this damage.
I am your number one fan,
And the least I can do is dedicate my time to cover your wounds
with my bare hands.

O mighty Moon,
When mankind sleep at night, you are coruscating.
My eyes won't dare to close themselves to sleep.
No one can ever comprehend the amount of love I have for you,
For it is myself that could never discern the reasons to all my
feelings.

Mistreated Queens

15/03/15

"I love you." He addressed me by choice.
"No, you don't," I replied back with a pity voice.

Love does not mean being manipulated in an unfairly manner.
Now days Queens have been treated with tribulation,
And now they're lost in between lies that lead to trauma.

How unfortunate that they've been welcomed into tormentation.

Precious Little Thing

15/03/15

Oh no,
I did it again.
I lost myself—again.

What have I done to the person I used to be?
Ever since love took hold of me, I've become unclear about its meaning
I've been searching the streets to find any answer
Now my lungs are affected by pollution
And my soul has weared its way into numbness."

My heart, it shattered from the amount of holes that have clattered around inside me for years.
No love, no lover can connect back these broken pieces
And if someone with the correct answer knocks on my door
I would rather him not.
The thing is I can never give my whole to someone: because I am not whole to start with.

So, dear lover, stay a stranger to me.
Admire this precious little thing—in your dreams.

Me

15/03/15

My hair, he hasn't seen.
My lips, they have never been kissed.
My face is clear from his fingerprints.
And my body, it has never been touched by a he.

Author

15/03/15

If I was told to write a book about the way you make me feel,
I would publish a book filled with blank papers
Because there is not even one word to describe the way you
make me feel.
And I don't know if that's a good or bad thing.

Two Selves

21/03/15

Stuck in between my two selves,
The lady who smiles in the day and the girl who cries at night.
Moon, lead me;
I am lost.
Pull me up when I'm feeling down.
My thoughts, they rush as I sink in my bed of lies.
Moon be my saviour.
Can't you see me,
Waving my hands as I drown?

I listened to you. I made sure in the day that my smile lit up the
entire town.
But when the sun decided it was time for it to back down,
I couldn't handle its rejection.
I cried for hours, begging it to stay up and out.
Now I'm lying in bed,
Deceitful about what I subliminally said.

A mask I wear.
"You're beautiful!" they tell me.
My face is a lie.
I'm nothing but a burning fire.
Don't believe this miserable heart of mine.
If I let you in, you are not able to love me for more than an hour.
I am sorry for everyone I have done wrong.
Whether it's your or my fault,
I take the blame, for I am the one to blame.
I am still fighting battles for the people I love yet cannot name.

I'm hurting, I'm hurting.
I'm crying as I write this phrase.
I know I've lost the people I tried loving all these days.
It's not okay; it's a problem. I'm swallowing down demons served
on a plate
I'm sorry, I'm so sorry anyway,
For being a silly monster who lives afraid.

The Mysterious Taste of Cinderella

23/03/15

If I stumble across you,
Tame me to your heart.
Enlighten me with one silky touch.
I want to be promised nothing but your love.

When your soft fingers run through my hair, I feel a sudden rush.
It's the feeling of blood galloping up these veins of mine.
To kiss you, that's a crime,
But rebellious defines me, and that's completely fine.
Your lips taste like red velvet cupcakes, but your tongue, it tasted like wine.
The clock is ticking. You tell me nothing as you ran to your destination before night hit the time.

Cinderella, don't leave me—you look so divine!
Does she love me, or am I the one who has fallen mysteriously in love with her crystal blue, lying eyes?

Icy Heart

25/03/15

What responsibility do you wear?
After mistreating such a beautiful young lady out of care …
Her tears are girt by tears.
All the choices you made were so unfair.
She attempted to cook and sauté the selfish ego you had served bare,
Unaware that nothing could possibly defrost such an icy heart you wear.

Your heart can only survive in the cold;
That's why when she tried to guide you into rehabilitation, and wanted you to travel a little in her world for some help,
You disrespected her.
Or maybe the pride you shared
Couldn't cope with living life under the sun's flare.

Hey, Mister,
As she lays here dead, in the middle of crying clouds and the warm-coloured sunset,
Tell me, what responsibility do you wear?

No Dignity

28/03/15

I surrendered,
Surrendered myself to you
I diagnosed him with power, and in return invigoration took over
whom?
The regret
Crawling beneath my breath …
A mere feeling, encapsulated in my throat.
Invigoration you wear as a coat
The power you have over me is in comparison with a remote.

How waggish of me to let such a puerile mind control my
emotions.
Nothing but witless, I felt.
You stole my dignity.
An imprudent thief defines you as a self.
Something that is mine cannot elevate you,
So give me back my dignity;
Without it, I am frivolous.
A pitch-black hole I invest time in, and portray myself as a whole.

The exterior of that hole may not have looked appealing,
However the interior atmosphere welcomed me with comfort—
that's for sure.
Looks can be deceiving,
And I shall swear by that until forevermore.

Embarrassing Lover

05/04/15

When I write,
His face is the first thing my eyesight is able to recognise.
Some days I cry from being able to see such a thing;
Other days, the voices in my head will drop heavily out of my mouth.
Most of the time,
I remember how much I loved him,
That I miss every part of the day he said "I love you" to me.
Then I think of how embarrassing and humiliating it all was, and I write it down regardless.

Counting Meteorites

07/04/15

Once upon a phase, I used to open my curtains
And try to count the meteorites on the moon, until my eyes were
unable to stay wide awake.
That was my nightly routine.

Now,
When the sun sets;
I scamper expeditiously to my room,
Close all my curtains, making sure no light peaks in between the
gaps,
And lay in my bed listlessly.
As the moon shines,
I am petrified to re-count the never-ending meteorites.

It's on my mind.
I constantly rethink how the connection between the moon and
me ended.

What is fate?
This is fate.

The Carved Diamond

08/04/15

He is mind-boggling.
However, I wish he noticed me.
But I'm just another girl sitting inside her room, so lonely,
Like a bird stuck in a cage.
A staggering diamond in my heart is well placed.
Nobody knows
Except the jeweller who carved it into that space.

It was customised to shine bright on my darkest days.
After all, I didn't realise it had captured such a soul's attention
from miles away.
I spent days before counting my blessings,
Now he's knocking on my front door,
Pleading for a position, to live with me a new life.

White Bedsheets

09/04/15

I sleep with uncovered bedsheets. It's skin, the colour of white divine.
If people entered my room; they won't get my art.
It'll confuse them, thinking that I'm such plain character.
However, I am much more than that—
A teenager replenished with so much life.

This uncovered bedsheet of mine does far more than you think.
It lugs happiness into my soul.
When the six a.m. sun beaming rises, glaring right through my window, its colour gives exotic texture to the bedsheet.

At eleven p.m., as the moon laughs with visible light, delivering hope into my bedroom in the midst of the night,
These white sheets you claim to be boring shall laugh with lustre and bring joy to my mind while reading me a bedtime story good night.

Don't ever underestimate white sheets,
For they are capable of bringing much more colour than you think at the right time.

Printed in the United States
By Bookmasters